Chronicles in Passing

Carol Smallwood

Foreword

Prolific author Carol Smallwood's latest poetry collection, *Chronicles in Passing*, stitches the scientific, the imaginary, and the mundane together into unique patterns, like the "Homemade Quilts" that one poem instructs us to make. Another piece titled "There Were Only" ends with lines that could be a mission statement for the entire project:

I lift my face to capture the rain of childhood and failing,
remember the earth is covered mostly with water and we
know less about oceans than the moon. So many wonders
lost in grade school.

For these poems are trying to sieve everyday wonders from the detritus of advertising, commerce, housework (an entire poem gives very practical rhyming instructions on how to hang up washing!), and other bits of data that we adults arrogantly call "facts".

The grown-up speaker of the opening poem, "A Moment Like No Other," remembers when she believed—and when she stopped believing—the nun's grotesque warning that children who talked in her class would fall through the floorboards to Hell. One thrilling, impossible-seeming realm of "fact" gives way to another, the infinite cosmos revealed by the new saints of modern science— Giordano Bruno, Carl Sagan, Neil deGrasse Tyson. What is gained, and what is lost, by this paradigm shift? A writer living in the world that technology has wrought, Smallwood must mount her own heretical resistance against the forces of disembodied data and language-twisting advertising.

One way she re-enchants the world is through poetic formalism—dignifying topics like supermarket flyers, hospital meals, and tax preparation by describing them in the form of a pantoum, sestina, rondeau, or triolet. This method builds a bridge, however tenuous and subjective, from banal modernity to a classical past where (we nostalgically imagine) it wasn't so hard to find "solid proof you're important and know what's real" ("Store Flyers"). As she concludes wistfully in "Select Moments":

Surely if I stood tall as possible
Long enough, tried hard enough
there'd come hints, some pattern?

—Jendi Reiter, author of *An Incomplete List of My Wishes: Stories* (Sunshot Press, 2018) and editor of *WinningWriters.com*

Introduction

Chronicles in Passing is a collection of formal and free verse poems about the incredible, enduring power of the written word to capture and preserve thoughts, emotions, and events. The word chronicles, associated with being a factual written account of history and record keeping, is used for contrast with classroom early reader words like "see Spot run," yet both reflect the times they were written. We remember encountering *Beowulf, Canterbury Tales,* and *Hamlet*—struggling to understand the strange words and culture and can but wonder what those following us will think about us. Chronicles are written by a select group (usually the winners), so caution is advised; individuals do not see things the same (remember the fable about each of the blind men describing an elephant)? And women were left out in the earliest days from the realm of scribes involved with keeping track of commerce of the Sumerians around 3200 BC and are still involved in catching up.

Examples of the formal poetry in the collection are: Rondeau—"An Unlikely Introduction;" Cinquain—"Neil deGrasse Tyson;" Pantoum—"Shallow Boxes;" Triolet—"A Supermarket Triptych;" Villanelle—"Unconscious Censor;" Sestina (without meter)—"A Regular." I find writing in formal style enjoyable and now view them like presenting a box wrapped in special paper with a bow: giving readers something extra. There are times though, that words in free verse work better in conveying the intended message. Also, what works as a villanelle will not as a triolet and as such, perhaps is better as free verse—so all one can do is try what fits like Goldilocks. Sometimes grasping for the right words ends in the Unfinished File, or in the full Trash Icon. It is hoped you will enjoy reading the poems as much as I have had writing them.

The nearly seventy poems are grouped by: Prologue; Part I; Part II; Part III; Epilogue. A sincere thanks to the foreword writer: Jendi Reiter, author of *An Incomplete List of My Wishes: Stories* (Sunshot Press, 2018) and editor of *WinningWriters.com*; and the blurb writers: Evan Mantyk, President, *The Society of Classical Poets,* Mount Hope, New York; Robert Fanning, Professor, Central Michigan University: author of *Severance; Our Sudden Museum; American Prophet; The Seed Thieves*; Mike Foldes, Founder/Executive Editor, *Ragazine;* Carolyn Howard-Johnson, *The New Book Review Editor;* multi award-winning writer; Carole Mertz, reviewer and essayist, contributor to such magazines as: *Mom Egg Review, The Ekphrastic Review, South 85 Journal*; Kathleen Christy, MLS, Adult Services Manager, Blount County Public Library; Jacqueline Berger, professor of English at Notre Dame de Namur University in Belmont, California, has had poems on *Garrison Keillor's Writers Almanac;* Dr. Mary Langer Thompson, *Poems in Water.*

"Poetry is not what words say but what is said between them, that which appears fleetingly in pauses and silences."
—Octavio Paz

Contents

Chronicles in Passing

Prologue

A Moment Like No Other

One day in reading class with "see Spot run," came the word, "suddenly;" it was in a room with a Sisters of Mercy nun who said if we talked the wood floor boards would separate and we'd fall into Hell.

Seeing the word, hearing, pronouncing "suddenly" as if tasting endless possibilities in adult words was a moment like no other—and I knew something had changed: being confined had vanished I was invincible.

Years later viewing Carl Sagan's revised *Cosmos* when an imprisoned Bruno (soon to be burned for heresy) mentally escapes into the infinity of space in which he believes, this invincibility became clear.

Part I

Waking Up

I leave
my other
self sleeping
to capture
dreams
when fresh

But pen
in hand,
they tumble,
turn to
dust
upon the
landing

A Hardcover Book

Carrying a hardcover book instead of a small electronic tool
I get polite, benevolent smiles seemingly reserved for the old;
people ask, "How old's your Bible?" as if following some rule.

I'm asked it so often I'm disappointed if not asked—you'll
find it easy to believe it could be true in any size household—
carrying a hardcover book instead of a small electronic tool

even admitting the chances low of it happening when polled.
Please assume I'm still thinking straight, am OK, all told;
people ask, "How old's your Bible?" as if following some rule

they learned most likely long ago quite young in grade school
and became very comfortable, complacent, following the fold.
Carrying a hardcover book instead of a small electronic tool

is not quite correct and some may frown, see you the fool,
quite the dinosaur, out of touch and even speckled with mold:
people ask, "How old's your Bible?" as if following some rule

that one should flow with the crowd—not intending to be cruel.
But I'll continue to read instead of text and not be controlled:
carrying a hardcover book instead of a small electronic tool
people ask, "How old's your Bible?" as if following some rule.

Store Flyers

They greet you each week by sliding entrance doors,
neatly folded paper in multiple colors always bold:
Back to School, Weekly Specials, at times on floors
written by experts to bring you into their family fold.

Neatly folded paper in multiple colors always bold
solid proof you're important and know what's real
written by experts to bring you into their family fold.
The words convince they have the best possible deal—

solid proof you're important and know what's real
including the exact amount you'll save as a consumer.
The words convince you they have the best possible deal
offering current "Buy 5 and Get 1 Free" with humor

including the exact amount you'll save as a consumer.
Back to School, Weekly Specials, at times on floors,
offering current "Buy 5 and Get 1 Free" with humor
they greet you each week by sliding entrance doors.

The Blue of Swimming Pools

With power out—people were stocking water and ice:
I thought it wise to drive to town.
The stoplights weren't working but people were polite,
it looked the same; the only grocery open was Brown's.

I thought it wise to drive to town.
People were pushing carts, nothing was different,
it looked the same—the only grocery open was Brown's;
the store had power but customers looked indifferent

people were pushing carts, nothing was different.
I checked on ice, thoroughly enjoying the cool air.
The store had power but customers looked indifferent;
it was good to be out and it was hard not to stare.

I checked on ice, thoroughly enjoying the cool air
stocking things that didn't require refrigeration.
It was good to be out and it was hard not to stare,
not to laugh at the tabloid photo of alien navigation

buying things that didn't require refrigeration.
The small alien carrying a limp woman made it impossible
not to laugh at the tabloid photo of alien navigation.
The bags of ice were colder than I thought possible;

the small alien carrying a limp woman made it impossible,
quite beyond belief. The letters on the ice were blue,
the bags of ice were colder than I thought possible;
the fleeting pleasures of hot days can be very few.

Quite beyond belief, the letters on the ice were blue,
soothing, the blue of swimming pools, hills of snow,
the fleeting pleasures of hot days can be very few.
With lots of water and ice I leave Brown's in the know:

soothing, the blue of swimming pools, hills of snow.
The stoplights weren't working but people were polite,
with lots of water and ice I leave Brown's in the know
with power out—people were stocking water and ice.

Lines Composed for the Day

The roads today
 were tape measures laid in
circles on a round earth formed
by shifting tectonic plates.

Poor Richard's Almanac revised:
    "Pay what you owe,
and you'll have no credit."

Actuary tables
    are now so easily available
online I do not look—consider them
lately as having become incorrect.

"What then, is time?"
    asked St. Augustine. "If no one
asks me, I know; if I wish to explain
to him who asks, I know not."

Homemade Quilts

Homemade quilts are never the same
And most made aren't for any fame;
Recycling your old clothes is wise:
Robes, jackets, sweatshirts, dresses, ties…
Not to include dishcloths a shame.

Some could be heirlooms to proclaim
Getting Antiques Roadshow acclaim
Becoming treasures in disguise—
Homemade quilts are never the same.

Don't look on quilting as a pain
It's good economy, tasteful gain;
Start out simple with a twin-size
Cut pieces straight—don't compromise
And sew a label with your name:
Homemade quilts are never the same.

"The Place of the Cure of the Soul"

is believed to have been written above the shelves
of the magnificent library of Alexandria, Egypt,
a major center of scholarship from the 3rd century
BC until it completely burned in 30 BC. My first
experience with libraries was in the early 1950's,
with many stairs to reach a Carnegie public library

built in 1908 with a fireplace and solid oak library
tables next to newspapers and magazines. It served
until 1966 when new accessibility laws resulted in
a one story building with a huge plate glass front
without imposing many stairs to reach the door.
My next library was in college: two-story ivy

with many classical white statues: required books
were brought from the stacks by busy student library
workers; you carried the books to tables to use if you
couldn't take them out—if you could, you had them
two weeks. It was a crowded center; two new ones
were built the last I heard and now probably more.

The sense of loss when all the papyrus scrolls were
burned in 30 BC is something I still can't forget
and at times wonder how culture would've changed
if they hadn't. What tragedy to have seen the library
burn and be unable to save it—yes, you think it could
never happen with our technology today. Information

has so proliferated that the sheer quantity begs for the
electronic version, a transition as profound as printing
in the times of Gutenberg. As a librarian I've had the
responsibility of making the change in accessing books
from the card catalog to online; magazines for library
appeared on CD's, print encyclopedia sets screamed age.

14

Yet, there's still something satisfying about the feel of books, the crackle of newspapers, smell of magazines and in owning them. What is the future of the library as the preservers of learning and culture? Paper trails are at times the only trail and local libraries the primary source for genealogists, biographers. Will computers

maintain our magnificent experience and knowledge, save its destruction, present a balanced scholarship— above all our human reach, "the Cure of the Soul."

The Pleiades

There is a tale of seven sisters whose father held up the sky
pursued by Orion, carried to the heavens by Zeus.
Farming season began when their star cluster appeared high—
their position in the fall marked change in seafaring use.

Pursued by Orion, carried to the heavens by Zeus.
Among the first stars mentioned in ancient Chinese annals,
their position in the fall marked change in seafaring use—
with the Native American Kiowa taking similar channels.

Among the first stars mentioned in ancient Chinese annals
written around four thousand years ago—and as a myth
with the Native American Kiowa taking similar channel—
including the seven maidens climb to Devil's Tower Monolith.

Written around four thousand years ago—and as a myth,
farming season began when their star cluster appeared high.
Including the seven maidens climb to Devil's Tower Monolith
there is a tale of seven sisters whose father held up the sky.

Counting Backwards

Counting backwards for anesthetic, the chatter near Christmas Day
was what was the favorite fruitcake among the surgeon and the rest—
the topic was nuts and raisins—but couldn't manage to have a say.

The next surgery happened the day after Christmas, the timing may
make you wonder but having it during vacation was wisest, the best:
counting backwards for anesthetic, the chatter near Christmas Day

was lively and spirited among the gowned staff excessively gay,
full of holiday joy as the sprig of evergreen on my tray to show zest.
The topic was nuts and raisins—but couldn't manage to have a say.

I walked around soon but recovery just dragged in the hospital stay
and the cheerfulness and fruitcake made me frown more I confess.
Counting backwards for anesthetic, the chatter near Christmas Day

was irritating, but was told it was just feminine hormone delay
and before long it would be better so wisely didn't reply if addressed:
the topic was nuts and raisins—but couldn't manage to have a say.

Yes, it all worked out in time but I avoid fruitcake even on a tea tray
which is something you probably might have already guessed.
Counting backwards for anesthetic, the chatter near Christmas Day—
the topic was nuts and raisins—but couldn't manage to have a say.

Anticipation

"Long day" someone said walking by with a sigh;
closing my eyes, I saw my preparer toss up everything
after all the shuffling, sorting—she just let forms fly
and left me there to gather what held my folder: string
from some package tied to a smiley face key ring.

Money conversation filtered from nearby but good guys
didn't listen so studied the floor of gray and beige rings
becoming Alice ready to have a white rabbit rush by.
Watching the computer with the tax preparer to satisfy
if forms were progressing, I settled on a Highland Fling

after I was out the door hoping the charge wasn't high
but each year it steadily rose—still, soon it'd be spring.
When would the unmistakable spring rain come down
or would it be imperceptible drizzle on the way to town
so one didn't expect amazing change it would bring?

The Hovering

The Fates in Greek mythology worthy of fame are three sisters;
deities who spin, determines the length of our thread, and snips it—
images we have most likely thought about, heard their whispers
saw ourselves dangling dangerously high over a deep pit.

Deities who spin, determines the length of our thread, and snips it—
defined in other cultures as weavers of destiny on tapestry loom:
saw ourselves dangling dangerously high over a deep pit;
also there's Macbeth's Three Witches so popular in classroom.

Defined in other cultures as weavers of destiny on tapestry loom,
images we have most likely thought about, heard their whispers—
also there's Macbeth's Three Witches so popular in classroom.
The Fates in Greek mythology worthy of fame are three sisters.

The Aura of Ballroom Dancing

Ah, the freedom, the grace of ballroom dancing (called dancesport if competitive) with a partner: costumes varying with the graceful waltz or the hectic jive—from ballet grace, to fast shimmy. From Prague, Copenhagen and around the world so many cities have competitions and festivals. The flirting, grace, fire—so much energy in the intricate steps

making two people appear one. In the pasa doble steps reminiscent of *Carmen*, my eyes feast on gorgeous dresses with sequins, feathers, ribbons, flounces: some I admit are designed a bit brief but others flow in spectacular neon hues. With their hair, makeup, shoes, one cannot help wondering how much dancers have invested and where

they buy such costumes and what keeps them securely in place. The slim men (mostly in black) do their steps sometimes in appealing coattails or mesh tops, sport an occasional unbuttoned shirt with jewelry—not showing much skin so must get hot dancing. How women dance in heels is a wonder but one must admit they look more graceful than those that don't but perhaps it's my hidden enjoyment of knowing they must be uncomfortable—reminiscent of being told "Suffer to be beautiful" when young. Both men and women's steps don't get their sleek hair out place. Some improvisations bring back P.G. Woodhouse's story of the newt owner demonstrating how a male newt attracts a female newt which his club friends adopt into a dance craze.

The men tend to purse lips, grimace, as if conveying passion;
women smile, many are tan with bare backs and arms—
long platinum hair is a plus. Yet no matter their steps,
I wonder about their relationship, judge their expertise.
Some partners never look at each other but dance as one;
others express much passion but don't dance like a couple.
It is fun to see child partners in dance costume perform
on programs like *America's Got Talent;* there's
competitions for nonprofessionals and younger dancers
such as the World Youth Champions for those under 21.

Yes, ballroom dancing from the waltz with ballet grace,
to the fast shimmy has energy, glamour—and romance.

Passage Triptych

Each time I enter, the feel is different: is it the conversation
or light from the windows? I come the same time every day
to look at the menu, order the same leafy vegetation.
Each time I enter, the feel is different: is it the conversation
that soothes, bestowes a needed daily validation
keeping me apart and yet letting me be part of the fray?
Each time I enter, the feel is different: is it the conversation
or light from the windows? I come the same time every day.

My cup today was Happy Meal size—an open book
with pictures of flying things filled with melting ice.
It is good to have a place to go once a day and not cook;
my cup today was Happy Meal size—an open book.
I've made a booth under a hanging lamp my own nook
where I study passing customers who seldom look twice.
My cup today was Happy Meal size—an open book
with pictures of flying things filled with melting ice.

Leaving, I saw the store's name plainly on the floor,
large letters from the lobby window blocked by sun
and would check for them tomorrow near the door.
Leaving, I saw the store's name plainly on the floor
like sundials our ancestors widely set such store—
marking the sun's passage was very widely done.
Leaving, I saw the store's name plainly on the floor,
large letters from the lobby window blocked by sun.

Why Wait Another Day

Feeling irritable, jittery or just plain restless?
Not getting all you can from each new day?
Join the crowd who've discovered Eurapress:
a side effect may bring on rapid tooth decay.

Not getting all you can from each new day?
Call the toll-free number now for a free trial:
a side effect may bring on rapid tooth decay.
Why wait another day when you can just dial.

Call the toll-free number now for a free trial
Do it for your better half and avoid regrets—
why wait another day when you can just dial
stop feeling short tempered, smoking cigarettes.

Do it for your better half and avoid regrets:
it could bring on insomnia, TB, chronic pain;
stop feeling short tempered, smoking cigarettes.
Make that call! Think of all you have to gain!

It could bring on insomnia, TB, chronic pain—
join the crowd who've discovered Eurapress:
make that call! Think of all you have to gain—
feeling irritable, jittery or just plain restless?

Father of History 484 BC-425 BC

Herodotus is chronicled as the first to arrange history a systematic way
and yet what he compiled is in quite an entertaining format and style
that also borrowed on traditional story-telling and myths it is safe to say.

Born in the Persian Empire, his name is still highly regarded, a mainstay
in the study of history—*The Histories*, regarded as written without guile:
Herodotus is chronicled as the first to arrange history a systematic way.

His writing on the Greco-Persian Wars, the long collision of which may
be read as accounts in the clash between East and West enmity or bile
that also borrowed on traditional story-telling and myths it is safe to say.

The Roman, Cicero, called him "The Father of History" in his day
which has remained despite much investigation, discussion, and trial:
Herodotus is chronicled as the first to arrange history a systematic way.

His writing explores lives of famous men, and battles holding much sway
such as Marathon, Thermopylae, with geographical digressions in miles
that also borrowed on traditional story-telling and myths it is safe to say.

Historians praise his historiographic narrative in classes to this day
encouraging some specialists to question his work, continue to rile:
Herodotus is chronicled as the first to arrange history a systematic way
that also borrowed on traditional story-telling and myths it is safe to say.

Shopping Today

While walking around to see which aisle had the strongest overhead fan,
I saw a sign: SALE $7.99 and under: $7.98—so small it was hard to read;
then counted how many there were of Extra Virgin Olive Oil brands
and wondered why I never had any recipes using flour made of flaxseed.

I saw a sign: SALE $7.99 and under: $7.98—so small it was hard to read
while sipping courtesy coffee said to have a nutty taste good with cream
and wondered why I never had any recipes using flour made of flaxseed.
The grocery store wasn't large but unfailingly seemed a familiar dream.

While sipping courtesy coffee said to have a nutty taste good with cream
it was fun to think myself a guest of honor of importance in the crowd:
the grocery store wasn't large but unfailingly seemed a familiar dream
a time to bask among the plastic plates, marshmallows, and feel endowed.

It was fun to think myself a guest of honor of importance in the crowd
then counted how many there were of Extra Virgin Olive Oil brands:
a time to bask among the plastic plates, marshmallows, and feel endowed
while walking around to see which aisle had the strongest overhead fan.

A Regular

Being greeted as a regular brought a smile. Grateful there's no line,
I bask in the familiar—the blast of ceiling air, the dent in the wall.
The wall menu seldom changes although panels sometimes are
dark from some light failure giving a disconcerting look of mourning
or separation until restored. The coffee comes in Limoges china,
the placemat not paper but linen, the tray sterling not dull plastic.

It was good to see what I'd ordered ready so fast on the plastic
tray while the ceiling music wasn't belting out lost love but
something else. I walked to my favorite table hoping it'd
be free and smiled when it was: employees called it "Your Table"
carrying trays sometimes for me. Putting the tray down as a
claim, I went to wash my hands using the wall soap dispenser

carefully as it wobbled; the water lukewarm; the sink had rust
but was clean with a striped straw and black spoon, both plastic
from someone and tried to picture who as the overhead air vent
blew a low comfortable note in competition with the hand dryer
on the wall. A woman trailing toddlers entered so retreated
to my table with clean hands. The window for fries is short

before becoming limp; ice keeps drinks cold just so long; burgers
are best eaten hot. There's a hum of shakes being made, a closing
of doors, and brush off the crumbs wondering who had eaten
there before and what they'd thought about. Did they use plastic
straws or just drink from cups, use catsup and salt on fries or go
solo—eating them all first? Did they sit alone or were they with

others? Did they study the faces on the placemat and read the
print on the back? Sometimes placemats were blank on the back
and I tore them into pages after folding: the paper tore well even
if it was thin. I brought placemats home to recycle perhaps
from guilt for daily using so many fast food things made of plastic
that weren't recycled but wished they were. Some places had

clear, some fast food places had black dishes of almost similar size. I'm wished a wonderful day from someone at the counter when I go, grant a Queen Elizabeth nod. Returning my dark plastic tray I noticed its salt sprinkles made a vast night sky full of wonder and understood why our ancestors made stories of constellations. Once outside, the scent of cigarettes—but no one was in sight.

Maybe there will be some new item on the menu that will delight: I'm a regular and will get a new placemat that may be different.

An Unlikely Introduction

I recall it: a poem in school
That sounded funny, had no rule
Told by second grade nun in black
Who never tolerated flack
And made it seem like April Fools.

Still it's known Edward Lear is cool
And sailing a "pea-green boat" you'll
Find yet to read in paperback…
I recall it.

"A runcible spoon" is a jewel
Although now you'd get ridicule
So best to be quiet—hold back;
Could "a Bong-Tree" make a comeback?
Nonsense: a nun's way to retool
I recall it.

On the Way

from town today there was a square large field, all white
dazzling under a late summer sky with Queen Anne's Lace:
near Gary's Funeral Home, lace flooded the field with light—
the celebration of such delicate abandon seemed out of place.

Dazzling under a late summer sky with Queen Anne's Lace
after the new addition to the County Commission on Aging
the celebration of such delicate abandon seemed out of place:
under lofty rolling cumulus August clouds a brash staging.

After the new addition to the County Commission on Aging
edged by a rim, a gray cemetery of felled trees by the woods,
under lofty rolling cumulus August clouds a brash staging:
an unexpected stranger on the outskirts of the neighborhood.

Edged by a rim, a gray cemetery of felled trees by the woods
near Gary's Funeral Home lace flooded the field with light—
an unexpected stranger on the outskirts of the neighborhood:
from town today there was a square large field, all white.

Select Moments

There was a time not long ago
Striving to feel the Earth turn
I spread like a child making
Snow angels on summer grass:
Couldn't one see clouds move?

I strained to detect movement
Like a forked divining rod
Searching for water despite
Reason saying it would be
Impossible even if rotating
Thousands of miles an hour
and circling the Sun.

Further back in years, I stared
A long time at a particular spot
One night at stars that appeared
Extra close waiting for any
Clues what it was all about.

Surely if I stood tall as possible
Long enough, tried hard enough
there'd come hints, some pattern?

Hanging Clothes on Clotheslines

Save energy instead of using dryers like most others do—
before using lines wipe with a clean damp cloth each time,
hang sheets so they block clothes you prefer others not to view.

Wash on the traditional Monday and don't be afraid of dew:
no matter your age, if you work fulltime, or aren't in your prime—
save energy instead of using dryers like most others do.

Pin up shirts by their tails, pants by cuffs, even if doing a few
and it is best to hang them so they're quite dry by dinnertime;
hang sheets so they block clothes you prefer others not to see.

Be neat and remove clothes pins to avoid them gathering grime,
and it's fine to use one pin instead of two if you only have a few.
Save energy instead of using dryers like most others do.

Pin up socks by the toe; keep hanging clothes—follow through
as they stand straight when harvesting frozen in wintertime:
hang sheets so they block clothes you prefer others not to view.

Do try this advice as you'll find it is solid, tested, and quite true
and you'll find taking clothes down also a relaxing pastime.
Save energy instead of using dryers like most others do—
hang sheets so they block clothes you prefer others not to view.

There Were Only

a few lights on in the library, no car tracks in the parking lot,
a gentle rain reinforcing the nose as the most elemental of
the senses. It was a much-needed rain that could be too late
for crops—a neighbor saying corn ears were very small.
So much rain early spring and then the lushness turns brittle.

Maybe there weren't any car tracks in the parking lot because
of the rain but when I reached the library, a couple said it was
closed. It was sad to think of computers blinking in the empty
library like solitary lighthouses.

I lift my face to capture the rain of childhood and failing,
remember the earth is covered mostly with water and we
know less about oceans than the moon. So many wonders
lost in grade school.

The New Galaxy

I'll always remember Aida: how the woman sitting
behind described how suddenly rain fell in Bermuda,
the rustle of programs, the excitement in a student's
voice about the discovery of a new galaxy—the warmth
of Mitchell's shoulder against mine for the first time
and basked in being a bird that'd found its way.

There was no mention of when I'd be returning home
on the broad balcony where we stood: I was a princess
with silver buttons being admired during intermission.
But the buried alive scene in the final act made me
whisper, "I can't stay. I'll wait outside." He stood with
me by the white Doric columns on the steps in the warm

night air until terror faded and panic of suffocation lost
its grip. I remembered smiling at the attendant when he
asked, "Did you and your wife enjoy the performance"
because it meant we looked like we belonged together.
The closed red and gold curtain seemed a sunset,
a final farewell, and clutched the program of Aida,

proof the night was real—and to stop tears, wondered
what the woman had looked like who'd described how
suddenly rain fell in Bermuda who'd sat behind us
wearing Estée Lauder and if she had season tickets
and would sit in the same seat in the theater—and
if she was happy. When Mitchell walked me to my

car in the darkness, his coat blew against me, a
benediction I knew had to be lasting. Would I ever
know the new galaxy the student had said with such
excitement had just been discovered?

Homemade Clothes

Bolts of store cloth of varied width lined shelves ready to
be taken, measured at a counter according to how many
yards the customer needed: as a child I watched bolts of
dark practical (serviceable) material uncoil for my mother.

Payment was by tubes whisked back and forth from an
upper story seemingly run by angels. Pattern catalogs
(dog-eared) were studied by her while I venerated white
ruffled eyelet, embroidered dimity, pastel taffeta.

New clothes for girls needed straight hems; the length
varied according to an annual pronouncement of fashion
strictly followed as a matter of course. Ready made
clothes were much preferred—homemade reminded
me of Laura in Little House on the Prairie books.

It was a serious time as pin after pin was attached
next to a yardstick as you stood on a chair and turned
when you were told. When done, getting out of the
new clothing was a tricky matter of not being jabbed.

Part II

Leaving My Drive

I noticed a wasp nest on
the end of a bare branch

Then there was another—
lanterns in autumn wind

As leaves fall they're in
my mind's eye during solitude

Dog Days Triptych

Ever wonder what the Dog Days of Summer are about?
The ancient Greeks needed to explain illness, storms,
fever, high temperature, war, disasters like drought.
Ever wonder what the Dog Days of Summer are about?
They are named for (Sirius) Dog Star, brightest no doubt
in the Canis Major constellation—brightness not the norm.
Ever wonder what the Dog Days of Summer are about?
The ancient Greeks needed to explain illness, storms.

I thought they were when dogs slept because it was so hot
and read it was translated into English about 500 years ago
covering July 3 to August 11, dates I was never taught:
I thought they were when dogs slept because it was so hot.
Grandmother often said, "Shake the yellow dog" I thought
to make one get rid of being lazy, stop going with the flow.
I thought dog days were dogs sleeping because it was so hot
and read it was translated into English about 500 years ago.

The constellation appears in Homer's *The Iliad* as the star
brightest at night being connected with suffering, disaster
named Orion's Dog: an evil visible point in the sky afar.
The constellation appears in Homer's *The Iliad* as the star
Sirius raising late in the dark liquid sky—a tale without par,
a classic for years and years of many a good school master.
The constellation appears in Homer's *The Iliad*, as the star
brightest at night being connected with suffering, disaster.

A Spider

was on the gas pump hanging by its line—
I knew it was a spider when it moved to the cement.
It was one of those black ones that jump,
a kind I never saw till moving to White Water.

When filling my tank I wondered if it were around
when gas was not yet oil before the sky was blue,
the smashing of asteroids and separating of continents,
the thunder of dinosaurs.

My tank full, I pushed a shopping list under it
and it went the other way; I moved the list and the
spider climbed by its line into a bag.

When home, I carried it to the woods where it caught
its line on waiting Queen Anne's Lace.

Dirt Roads

Dirt roads as reality checks are to be recommended:
sans grass, cement, asphalt, tar, they reveal
naturalness, a useful reflection to be commended—
the passage of seasons, time, what's real.

Sans grass, cement, asphalt, tar, they reveal
footprints, tire tracks, proof of what's been,
the passage of seasons, time, what's real
so plainly to make you dare glimpse within.

Footprints, tire tracks, proof of what's been
between plants nearly extinct growing by the road
so plainly to make you dare glimpse within
as the plants only grow there wild, unbowed.

Between plants nearly extinct growing by the road
the road sees rain, ice, snow come and go
as the plants only grow there wild, unbowed
while punctuated here and there with a crow.

The road sees rain, ice, snow come and go
holes keep appearing no matter how often graded
while punctuated here and there with a crow:
leafy arms of maple and elm make them shaded.

Holes keep appearing no matter how often graded,
a sure incentive for cars to slow down,
leafy arms of maple and elm make them shaded
while drivers bounce with varying frowns.

A sure incentive for cars to slow down,
the steady sound of rattling gravel as tires grip
while drivers bounce with varying frowns:
any day dirt road makes memorable trips.

The steady sound of rattling gravel as tires grip
naturalness, a useful reflection to be commended—
any day dirt road makes memorable trips;
dirt roads as reality checks are to be recommended.

Shifting Continents

Our continents once one, repeatedly separate, and join anew:
Pangea the most recent supercontinent, is the best known—
without national boundaries, state lines, circles of latitude.

Surrounded by water mostly in the southern hemisphere, the mood
must have been one of solitude without any boundaries or zones:
our continents once one, repeatedly separate, and join anew:

It would've been awesome to have been high in space to view
this huge supercontinent split and come back from the unknown
without national boundaries, state lines, circles of latitude.

What would've been the color of the sky—it wouldn't have been blue;
and how deep was Panthalassa the colossal ocean all on its own?
Our continents once one, repeatedly separate, and join anew.

Maps show South American, African coasts fit together—a shoo-in
and one of the marks of continental drift, plate tectonics backbone
without national boundaries, state lines, circles of latitude.

It is predicted our continents will again combine, become one (you
probably guessed) and all boundaries of states, nations, overthrown:
our continents once one, repeatedly separate, and join anew
without national boundaries, state lines, circles of latitude.

The Naming

Who would imagine names the Purslane family of weeds would include
Common Burdock, Horsenettle, Field Pennycress, and many more;
Wild Carrot more widely known as Queen Anne's Lace is in the brood.

Some young leaves like the Dandelion (lion's tooth) are a health food
and English Daisy, Milkweed can be found mentioned in popular lore:
who would imagine names the Purslane family of weeds would include?

The family also includes Poison Ivy creating its own kind of mood—
getting too close to this one may end up with a trip to the drugstore.
Wild Carrot more widely known as Queen Anne's Lace is in the brood.

Wild Strawberry, Nimblewill, Orange Hawkweed aren't what you'd
expect and Redroot Pigweed, Purple Deadnettle, are more to look for:
who would imagine names the Purslane family of weeds would include?

Silvery Thread Moss, Creeping Speedwell, Chickory, one can conclude
would be fun to identify—Prostrate Pigweed would be hard to ignore:
Wild Carrot more widely known as Queen Anne's Lace is in the brood.

It would have been great to have a chance to name one when viewed
walking on a summer day in a field, deep woods, or open rolling moor;
who would imagine names the Purslane family of weeds would include?
Wild Carrot more widely known as Queen Anne's Lace is in the brood.

T-Shirts at Wendy's

A girl carrying a baby in a sequin tutu t-shirt's read:
"Life is Like Toilet Paper, Your Either On A Roll Or
You're Out"

A laughing boy with, LOVE IS A, disappearing under
a black t-shirt with flame letters: "See You in Hell"

A woman staring into space in her thirties with a
silent young boy: "I Fear Nothing, I'm a Nurse"

A Pink Cinquain

Pink has become a favored cultural color, more subtle, less primitive than red:
black mixed with pink is considered seductive, innocent when used with white
and acquired its own name just in the late 17th century is what we read.
In the 1940s, blue for boys, pink for girls became the custom, an accepted rite;
Mamie Eisenhower's 1953 inaugural pink gown was a major fashion highlight

and Jacqueline Kennedy helped popularize pink, making it spread
while the famous painting, "Pinkie" symbolized youth in daylight.
There are amazing hues of pink in roses, dahlias, and hyacinths, in flower beds
varying hues of pink attract insects aiding pollination to be widespread.
Names for pink—cotton candy, cherry blossom pink, and fuchsia give delight;

tickled pink, seeing pink elephants, in the pink, are sayings that have spread.
Breast Cancer Awareness uses pink ribbons to stand out in the public limelight
with distinction to combat a wide health problem. In "Young Goodman Brown,"
Faith wears a pink hair ribbon to symbolize innocence; in *Little Women*, bound
ribbons appear on Amy's twins. All told—pink packs a lot of cultural insight.

Perspective

Not a Car

    was at the 4-way stoplight and
looked around in hopes of seeing
one, or even better—a cement
mixer in carnival colors.

    When the light turned, the rear
view mirror gradually telescoped
the stoplight until it faded in
little cat feet fog.

Before

    we used telescopes, one explanation was the
Sun was Apollo driving a chariot with horses
(they each had their own names) across the sky.

    Now we know the Sun's a chemical reaction
and there's many larger—but it's still more
satisfying to see it as Apollo and his horses.

When a Certain Age

    if you're a woman be prepared to be called
young lady, sweetheart, honey, dear as
terms of endearment; it's best not to recall
those you used for others not long ago.

As I Stood

aside, the surface of
the high white marble altar
of my childhood melted,
descended in wide loops
of lumpy gray without a sound—
and avoided seeing where the
statues, gilded spires, vases,
candles, carved Latin slipped.

The Washing

Even if the car wash line was long, yesterday's
was longer so had to stay as could no longer
consider graying windows as tinted.

After studying cloud patterns, there were 4 cars
behind me, 10 ahead: the place must be making
loads of money.

After using the vacuum there were 8 cars
behind and noticed more harried attendants
collecting money than usual.

Found my value coupons hard to remove
and my credit card to not hold up a line
taking on a sedate funeral aspect.

Once inside there was a calming scent of soap,
lulling pull between green octopus strips,
passing swirling blue brushes.

After a waterfall rinsing, towel attendants
emerged in the mist to finish my acceptably
clean car—for a few days.

A Supermarket Triptych

Did the passersby think I was a restaurant owner instead of there
to enjoy the colossal bags and jars Alice in Wonderland size?
A Motown tune belted out love and emotions—places I didn't dare.
Did the passersby think I was a restaurant owner instead of there
to wonder, check the sales, notice anything new, leisurely stare
as I sip my courtesy cup of decaf, speculate on good looking guys?
Did the passersby think I was a restaurant owner instead of there
to enjoy the colossal bags and jars Alice in Wonderland size?

The middle of supermarket aisles are good as neither side receives
preference like Queen Elizabeth's "walk abouts" among fans,
nodding to the Clabber Girl while sipping decaf, A.M. Reprieve.
The middle of supermarket aisles are good as neither side receives
a longer inspection than the other especially when one perceives
potato chips, chocolate on sale—best run to the aisle of pans.
The middle of supermarket aisles are good as neither side receives
preference like Queen Elizabeth's "walk abouts" among fans.

The grocery bottles of extra virgin oil stood in extra straight lines
on top shelves, labels maroon or yellow—the white delightfully prim
covering their round fronts facing aisles as if fashion runway designs.
The grocery bottles of extra virgin oil stood in extra straight lines
exotic, sophisticated, as if competing with bottles of imported wines
so not to be neglected, sidelined—relegated to bottom shelf confines.
The grocery bottles of extra virgin oil stood in extra straight lines
on top shelves, labels maroon or yellow—the white delightfully prim.

A Matter of Nightmares

Aunt Heidi said, "Bob hasn't been sleeping well
and his nightmares of Hiroshima are terrible."
She straightened her pile of crossword puzzles
and said, "I worry about him." Lily could smell
the insect repellent he had to spray before
going to sleep.

To delay going home, Lily told Aunt Heidi about
Alison's brother who'd returned from Nam:
unexpected sounds sent him diving under
any cover; certain smells made him shake,
his arms were infected trying to get rid of
"crawly leeches."

When Lily heard such things she felt so fortunate
she hadn't been a soldier, not realizing she had
post-traumatic stress disorder first called
shell shock: that what went on behind white
picket fences was war.

An American Icon

Blue jeans began in 1871: sturdy pants, duck cloth in brown
for miners using horse harness rivets to add strength necessary
for long wear, developing into eventual popularity world round.

A change to denim (a sturdy cotton twill) became a shakedown
when blue dye began the look we consider being customary;
blue jeans began in 1871: sturdy pants, duck cloth in brown.

A ribbing of diagonal design made a cloth that became renowned:
indigo makes the warp, the weft white, producing the shade vary
for long wear, developing into eventual popularity world round.

By 1960 blue jeans became high fashion, a designer meltdown
and collectors rivaled old gold prospectors in being monetary:
blue jeans began in 1871: sturdy pants, duck cloth in brown.

Then the distressed kicked in—the tattered, holes handed down
and patches haphazard; some mostly threads making them airy
for long wear, developing into eventual popularity world round.

Jeans now stretch but "tend to sag" after walking around town
my daughter said and may shrink when washed—quite arbitrary;
blue jeans began in 1871: sturdy pants, duck cloth in brown
for long wear, developing into eventual popularity world round.

Neil deGrasse Tyson

People Magazine voted him the "Sexiest Astrophysicist Alive" of his day;
acclaimed science communicator, multi-awarded, is easy on the eye
and like watching, listening to him—he captures admiration without delay
even if orbits, Einstein, telescopes, eclipses, equations about the sky
makes you wonder, shake your head and keep asking how and why.

Director of Hayden Planetarium in New York, admirer of Michael Faraday,
Isaac Newton, he talks of them like they're friends; he's a regular guy
a ballroom dancer, husband, father with speaking honors of highest sway—
a researcher with still the look of a college wrestler ready for any fray;
as a teenager he met the famous Carl Sagan always hard to classify.

He got the department for American Museum of Natural History underway
in astrophysics in 1997—one smiles at the various space pictures on his ties.
He worked with PETA issuing a public service message on animal kindness
and an interview to help diminish a long general widespread blindness.
Anticipation for his next program or book is a big highlight I can't deny.

Driving Into Town

pine trees skewered the snow—
frilled green cellophane toothpicks
next to slim bare-limbed trees
as if at a cocktail party.

Safety of Predictability

A lack of sleep encourages awareness in the safety of predictability:
you think of clocks, the rhythm of day and night—that total quiet is rare.
Sleeplessness encourages losing civility, a definite increase in irritability,
a fear others know what you're thinking and will banish you elsewhere.

You think of clocks, the rhythm of day and night—that total quiet is rare.
There's fear of the unknown, an uneasiness gravity will come to an end
a fear others know what you're thinking and will banish you elsewhere
and you fight the sinking feeling it could be the end—useless to pretend.

There's fear of the unknown, an uneasiness gravity will come to an end;
sleeplessness encourages losing civility, a definite increase in irritability
and you fight the sinking feeling it could be the end—useless to pretend.
A lack of sleep encourages awareness in the safety of predictability.

The Fashion Look

Exclusive, Alluring! Organic and spandex slouchy pants in black,
pond blue, early tulip; snug, reinforced elastic waist 2 inches wide:
no bulky pockets to detract your assurance of leading the pack.

Wear the slouchies with a divine jewel-neck swingy top, show knack
that's slimming, lightweight, in neon selected to get you eyed—
Exclusive, Alluring! Organic and spandex slouchy pants in black

features recycled materials. Don't miss our pencil skirt to bring back
the flattering mod, medi-length look in up to size 10: keep in stride
no bulky pockets to detract your assurance of leading the pack.

Another coordinated choice is our tee—a hot choice not off the rack
to be admired for its simple elegance with a choice of initials applied.
Exclusive, Alluring! Organic and spandex slouchy pants in black:

add our ankle boots and you'll not have to wait for quick feedback
fueled by sheer envy—the fashion combination can't be denied:
no bulky pockets to detract your assurance of leading the pack

also available in other colors. On the go? Just toss in your rucksack
with our swingy top or coordinated tee and let adventure be a guide!
Exclusive, Alluring! Organic and spandex slouchy pants in black
no bulky pockets to detract your assurance of leading the pack.

The Iliad

The Iliad, considered the earliest work in the Western literary tradition
is one of the most famous and loved chronicles recounting events in
the Trojan War, and Siege of Troy—chronicles used in later renditions.

Although usually attributed to Homer, *The Iliad* is an older addition
an inheritance of singer-poets—it's uncertain Homer ever lived, had kin:
The Iliad is considered the earliest work in Western literary tradition.

The poem's lines are dactylic hexameter, a formal rhythm audition
making it easier to memorize, some phrases are repeatedly akin…
the Trojan War, Siege of Troy—chronicles for other later renditions.

The theme is one of war and peace: a mix of horror, glory: submission
both of heroism and viciousness questioning the heavy cost of a win—
The Iliad, considered the earliest work in the Western literary tradition.

The many gods and goddesses mock or copy the human condition
are used as allegories, psychological purposes, for comedy built-in:
the Trojan War and Siege of Troy—chronicles used in later renditions.

Poems were recited at festivals and for those in important position
by singers beating the measure with staffs maybe covered by skin.
The Iliad, considered the earliest work in the Western literary tradition:
the Trojan War, and Siege of Troy—chronicles used in later renditions.

Part III

There Comes Such Days

There comes such days we turn back time
By a childhood nursery rhyme
Said in the midst of winter's night
Then fear the very rhyme outright
And turn distrustful of daytime.

Maybe all turns a pantomime
And tomorrow not worth the climb:
A "told by an idiot…" tale—
There comes such days.

How does sleep come in the meantime
Living under such pale moons? I'm
Sure many nights might have starlight
When midsummer dreams flood outright
After demure days of springtime—
There comes such days.

The Epic of Gilgamesh

It is generally accepted that the oldest epic in the world was written 1500 years before *The Iliad* making it a 4,000-years old founding text: *The Epic of Gilgamesh*. It's an account of a Sumerian, Gilgamesh, the hero king of Uruk, and his adventures. The tale was uncovered in the library of Ashurbanipal in Nineveh in 1853—written in 12 clay tablets in cuneiform; some say archaeologists found the chronicle

near Mosul, Iraq. The adventure-filled tale follows a hero's chronicle journal where he slays monsters, meets the gods, in his search for immortality. The epic began as several Sumerian poems and stories going back to 2100 B.C. and was lost after 600 B.C. until discovered in the 1800's. Gilgamesh is handsome, young, athletic: his mother was the goddess Ninsum and his father a priest-king, and this mixture

is reflected in the good and bad traits displayed. A survivor of the Great Flood, advises the young king in the second half of the chronicle to accept his mortality as he cannot change it and he returns to Uruk to rule wisely. Gilgamesh remained mostly unknown until the mid-twentieth century, but, since the late twentieth-century, it's become more and more popular with scholars and in current world literature.

Images of Aging

The pyramids for deceased rulers are the only famous Seven
Wonders of the Ancient World that've lasted. Aging is a finality
for others and not for me—by not looking in the mirror it won't
happen; something best handled with Emily Dickinson's slant.

I recall the shadows of three bent, shuffling men with canes and
cups in the James Bond film, *Dr. No;* they were only disguises
but were the incarnation of feeble, dependent, laughable old age
still many years away—I was in my twenties.

Before I aged, the elderly belonged to a group not needed, out
of touch with the times, to be tolerated. It was a surprise seeing
myself reflected in a store window and my hair looked like it
was snowing—then realized it was summer.

Three Greek deities increasingly come to mind: Clotho, who
spins the thread of life; Lachesis, who determines how long we
live; and Atropos, who cuts the thread with shears. As a quilter
I appreciate sharp shears and hope hers are—she's had practice.

Questions of the Day

Coffee Rub has salt, coffee, brown
sugar, paprika, chili peppers,
garlic, onions—but what's it for

How do spiders walk on ceilings

Why so many words for dying:
deceased, departed, croaked,
pushing up daisies, passed,
moved on, demise, expired,
gone, no longer with us, with
the angels

How well could you see with the
first mirrors—polished obsidian
stone

What's the best theory where
water comes from

When did bees begin using the
hexagon as the best shape to
store honey

Who wrote: "Life is Short;
Enjoy Your Trip" for the spare
tire cover on the car ahead

Triplet on Form

What circle of Dante's Purgatory has Keat's carved inscription:
"Beauty is truth, truth beauty. That is all ye know, and all ye
need to know?" Truth is more slippery for women as its from
what they see and feel—the ooze of living, blood of creation.

I heard that when a person falls between a passing train and
train platform their body is twisted like a corkscrew ribs down.
Friends are called as after they're removed they have a minute
or two to live—before that they're just numb.

I told Elizabeth's husband that when mowing it was so dry this
summer, "I'd never seen dust like that." When he said,
"It's never been so dry before," the logic, the mere acceptance
of saying things the way they were seemed crude, impolite.

The Perennial Sherlock

We first meet Sherlock Holmes through Dr. Watson just back from Afghanistan, and it's in London's Criterion Bar that Stamford links Watson with Holmes as a possible person to share rooms and as they say, the rest is history—the rooms at 221B Baker Street are still maintained. The first story I read, *The Adventure of the Speckled Band*, was in a freshman high school English class. Soon after I wrote lines

from *A Study in Scarlet* and often reread the memorable lines— "From a drop of water," said the writer, "a logician could infer the possibility of an Atlantic or a Niagara without having seen or heard of one or the other." Watson calls it "twaddle" only to learn Holmes was the writer. Watson was surprised Holmes didn't know the earth revolved around the sun: that he advised not filling your brain with

things you'll never use. My well-thumbed 1,122 page copy, *The Complete Sherlock Holmes*, with 1930 copyright begins with lines of the "In Memoriam Sherlock Holmes" essay by Christopher Morley: Doyle's work originally appeared in nine separate books. Sidney Paget is the most famous illustrator of Holmes stories defining our image of him in the Strand Magazine. So what does make one reread Holmes?

Sir Arthur Conan Doyle tells us little about Holmes but as readers we look for clues to what makes him tick. We carefully judge if Dr. Watson is a reliable narrator and glean clues as well about this ordinary doctor to tell us more about Holmes. What makes the lines so memorable about reading Doyle's stories is the atmosphere or world he manages to convey in a few words in which we become a part. The

villains seeking revenge are often better people than their victims. We see into English London and country life when the Empire played a large factor in British life as well as the world. There is the pull between staid Watson and mercurial Holmes, the varied official police reactions to Holmes. Characters of all classes are sharply drawn in lines full of atmosphere readers peruse for pleasure over and over again.

64

Movies and television offer a string of Sherlock Holmes as each generation fashions him in its own image. Even Spielberg has directed films on the detective. Stories like "Silver Blaze" have the well know lines about the dog not doing anything in the night, and Holmes concluding: "That was the curious incident." My set of videos features Jeremy Brett in an outstanding Holmes portrayal—but reading his words is still best.

Doyle's London and vivid settings still comes to life in every story and the 221B Baker Street remains a haven for adventure chronicles. I'm most grateful Holmes was in my freshman English textbook.

Spools of Thread

The spools are in a chest tray to keep them from falling out of sight mostly:
my favorite? A wooden spool marked "Fast to Boiling, Bel-Waxed, 15¢"…
there are others underneath quite likely but it's best not to search too closely.

The printing, Fast to Boiling, must mean the color won't turn ghostly
if boiled but am not sure what Bel-Waxed means or makes any sense.
The spools are in a chest tray to keep them from falling out of sight mostly.

There is also a Pure Silk, Button Hole Twist, 15¢ (Shade 9730) remotely
sea green on a wooden spool half the size the dusty rose thread, more dense.
There are others underneath quite likely but it's best not to search too closely.

Thread colors are especially a joy to explore during white winters, slowly
mixing them up on the tray—the handling probably not pure commonsense:
the spools are in a chest tray to keep them from falling out of sight mostly.

It is fun to wonder where they came from, if their times were that wholly
different from now, and if anyone else will claim them without pretense—
there are others underneath quite likely but it's best not to search too closely

and keeping thread handy for repairs is wise; I can say that plainly, boldly
treasure chests are of practical use as well as lifelong interest: a solid defense.
The spools are in a chest tray to keep them from falling out of sight mostly:
there are others underneath quite likely but it's best not to search too closely.

Defining Time

Time's illusive to understand, define
even with the definitions, planck and light years—
centuries studying, grasping design
a slippery concept to confront human fears.

Even with the definitions, planck and light years—
it goes slowly when we're young, fast when old
a slippery concept to confront human fears
involving our condition when all is told.

It goes slowly when we're young, fast when old
there's many known poems and quotations
involving our condition when all is told
making little sense after all the rotations.

There's many known poems and quotations,
centuries studying, grasping design
making little sense after all the rotations;
time's illusive to understand, define.

Two Roads

Frost's poem relates choosing the grassy road wanting wear
not the more traveled in the yellow wood when they diverged;
it's seemingly simple and presented by teachers as student fare.

For most of us it is a poem to recall when in an armchair
or perhaps during times when decisions have clashed and surged.
Frost's poem dwells on choosing the grassy road wanting wear

but is described as "a tricky poem" by Frost himself so be aware
and read the stanzas carefully so conclusions needn't be purged:
it's seemingly simple and presented by teachers as student fare.

Standing before two roads encourages one to visualize and stare
with the morning traveler where the undergrowth converged—
Frost's poem dwells on choosing the grassy road wanting wear.

"The Road Not Taken" is a work that most agree deserves fanfare
and a careful rereading of it shouldn't need to be urged:
it's seemingly simple and presented by teachers as student fare

although nine syllables per line (not eight) might've been a dare—
for most readers this diversion in meter's easily submerged.
Frost's poem dwells on choosing the grassy road wanting wear:
it's seemingly simple and presented by teachers as student fare.

A Time for Everything

When going to a doctor's appointment to hear the results of a test
retake in June, white puffs I'd never seen before drifted like snow
and wondered what seeds they were. Kids were hanging out at the
corner of Long's Funeral Home—some on bikes, some leaning
against utility poles.

I made a note of the location of the only place in town selling
Lady Godiva; if the news was bad, I'd buy loads of candy but not
look at any flowers for fear I'd see some wilting. Better yet—
have the boxes delivered—money wouldn't matter any longer nor
would calories or tooth decay: day after day of the best milk
chocolates in gold boxes that when empty, I'd pile in graceful
golden towers.

A time to be born, and a time to die;
A time to plant, and a time to uproot the plant.
A time to kill, and a time to heal;
A time to tear down, and a time to build.
A time to weep, and a time to laugh;
A time to mourn, and a time to dance.

Weren't they the words heard so often by folk singers in the
Seventies? If I were to die now I'd avoid being good for nothing;
I wouldn't tell Mark or Jenny because they had children to worry
about. At the end (before tiring of chocolates and videos) the
doctors would shoot pain stuff and I'd just drift away.

I had my death so pleasantly arranged down to the exact Estee
Lauder for lace-edged sheets that when the doctor told me I was
OK, there flooded a disconcerting thought of a trout defrauded
of a hovering mayfly.

Our Unconscious Censor

One can train to write down dreams just as soon you wake,
when all the myriad details are still fresh, new and clear as a bell—
yet is it best to let your built-in censor block when so much is at stake?

Waking up with chewed mouth, gnashing teeth deserves a double take
to try and figure out what's going on in your subconscious, not dwell:
one can train to write dreams down just as soon you wake

and confront the subterranean fear as if a waiting rattlesnake
coiled in a yawning cavern that's deeper, more terrifying than any hell:
yet is it best to let your built-in censor block when so much is at stake?

Dreams hover during day threaten to surface making for headaches
only to evaporate like dew. Why is uncovering such a hard sell?
 One can train to write down dreams just as soon you wake

so get rid of the hoary, deep oozing fear making you tremble, shake:
but your built-in censor is a trench against shattering bombshells—
yet is it best to let your built-in censor block when so much is at stake.

Is one a coward not to go ahead and capture dreams, face at daybreak
once and for all—end the fear—what could be that awful to dispel?
One can train to write down dreams just as soon you wake
yet is it best to let your built-in censor block when so much is at stake?

Blood Test in January

In the hospital waiting room covers share;
Time: Why Your DNA Isn't Your Destiny.
Newsweek: Yes He Can (But He Sure Hasn't Yet).

The television: Filibuster, 2,000 marines in Haiti.
The world looks to the U.S.

The woman across from me chewed bubble gum
under the clock with extra sharp hands near a sign:
We Ask for a Photo ID Prior to Providing Services.

A pink pillow with hearts supports my hand
after I'm called.

The young man tells me to make a fist and after
the jab asks, "Are you all right?"

"I'm fine," continuing to compare his shoelaces
through sunglasses.

On the way home, a police car blocks a funeral
procession: car after car with festive fluttering
flags in snow.

Month of December

The coming of the month of shortest days recalls the many
world wide stone structures made to mark the winter solstice.

Shamed to admit I just learned seasons are caused not by how
far earth is from the sun but how the axis tilts as the sun hits it.

It is the month when brushing my hair reminds me of Einstein's
due to static by the lack of moisture in the air.

Shallow Boxes

Quilting pieces, stacked in shallow cardboard boxes from a grocery store
to be ready when sleep eludes, each box with choices of cut up clothes—
protection like the Maginot Line against invasions of bad dreams, a war
fought by women with a needle to seem next day fresh as a primrose.

To be ready when sleep eludes, each box with choices of cut up clothes,
sandbag sewing scraps of twill, denim, wool, fleece, flannel, cotton:
fought by women with a needle to seem next day fresh as a primrose
after giving up tossing and turning—the past a jumble not forgotten.

Sandbag sewing scraps of twill, denim, wool, fleece, flannel, cotton:
protection like the Maginot Line against invasions of bad dreams, a war
after giving up tossing and turning—the past a jumble not forgotten:
quilting pieces, stacked in shallow cardboard boxes from a grocery store.

Sleep

A good night's
sleep is said to
enable leaps over
tall buildings.

But morning eyes
mirror boulders
inched up hill.

Shades of Limbo

The vertical line of spindles on the familiar bed headboard
were becoming visible—confirming a night without sleep.

Light slipped through closed blinds: the room getting form
where the ceiling ended and the wall began evident by
different shades of gray—the ghostly chair by the window
acquiring shape.

Perhaps it would be good to get up, end this limbo but
the lace edging you sewed to a sheet brings stability,
and you're grateful for a pen in your hand but wondered
if the words to describe where the door was would
be readable.

Earplugs make a black/white silent film, and getting up,
walk like Charlie Chaplin for courage.

Dragnet Revisited

Recently I ran across *Dragnet* on YouTube: the distinctive
music reinforced it was indeed the old police program I saw
years ago and was curious how it'd look today—Jack Webb
(Sergeant Joe Friday) as writer, actor, producer, director.
Each segment included "This is the city" identified as Los
Angeles (not L.A.), how large it was, the day of the week,

if it was warm, cold, or cloudy while panning the sprawling
city. Most programs I saw were in black and white and each
program began with the same picture of Badge 714, the iconic
tune, and a Jack Webb (I saw him smile once) telling it was
"day watch out of homicide" or another assignment and the
name of his male partner. It was reassuring that the story

(it was an award-winning radio series) would always uphold
justice. The cars and clothes were ones when I was young;
women resembling the cast in *I Love Lucy* answered doors
wearing aprons. The rising smoke of cigarettes was prevalent—
match covers used for clues or taking notes; cigarettes offered
with an occasional lighter; cigarettes praised by doctors, opera

singers in commercials. Jack Webb leaves a carton at the
hospital for his partner. Milk came in glass bottles; local
theaters had jackpots, cartoons, newsreels added to movies;
there was an absence of gays, lesbians, minorities, and women
in leadership roles. The smog was very evident but never
acknowledged. The phones were rotary; punch cards located

criminals who used flash paper to burn evidence. *Dragnet's* appeal includes not knowing when it's being serious—a hotel named, Dewey Arms, and "names have been changed to protect the innocent" part of the formula. The unmarried Webb remains unemotional and a partner who was a family man provided contrast an effective foil like Dr. Watson to Sherlock Holmes.

Dragnet lacks cases of rape, incest, domestic abuse unlike today's news of abuse in the workplace, Catholic Church, elected officials, movie stars, but it isn't unusual to see writer guidelines not accepting abuse topics. With social media becoming so popular, it'll be fascinating to see what changes it may bring—and what cultural elephants/taboos will be uncovered.

What Does it Mean?

"It is what it is" a clerk replied to my comment how busy she was last week.
Has it any meaning—could it be profound wisdom—or just another cliché?
There's something about the saying that's mysterious, illusive, unique—
is it a passing figure of speech soon dated, already has had its heyday?

Has it any meaning—could it be profound wisdom—or just another cliché?
Maybe what it means depends on a shrug, raised eyebrow, tone, or frown.
Is it a passing figure of speech soon dated, already has had its heyday?
Most likely my curiosity about the phrase will eventually just die down.

Maybe what it means depends on a shrug, raised eyebrow, tone, or frown.
There's something about the saying that's mysterious, illusive, unique—
most likely my curiosity about the phrase will eventually just die down.
"It is what it is" a clerk replied to my comment how busy she was last week.

A Matter of Rowing

It is the rule: the way to row
Is tradition set long ago
The old English river men way—
Not seeing ahead seemed okay,
Sitting backwards the way to go.

College sportsmen made it a show
For Americans to borrow
And it just became a mainstay...
It is the rule.

So over country that the crow
flys are scenes of the status quo:
Though rowers often may pray
Not to ram another causeway
and add another boating woe:
It is the rule.

An Ode

Professor Hedley was the first professor I saw in college. He taught History of Western Civilization, a required two-semester class. On a September morning, he entered the large classroom, cleared his throat as he looked over the packed room, went to open several high windows, before coming to the middle of the room where you could hear the proverbial pin drop. His sandals were the first I'd ever seen on a man; he wore socks but the shoes were sure enough sandals, and from the small town I came from, it was about the same as wearing a bathing suit.

Professor Hedley's reputation as a scholar was known—he'd debated Lewis Mumford and was a friend of Frank Lloyd Wright. I didn't know either of them but students said it with such awe, I knew they were luminaries of the highest order. I was to get to know Professor Hedley, meet his wife during the next few years, and he remained the only professor who pronounced my French surname correctly. When he quoted Shakespeare that morning, "sleep that knits up the ravel'd sleave of care," his obvious admiration of the lines put him on the same level as the great bard and it was like a dip into a pool, being made whole again.

Professor Hedley, besides exuding sophistication, made the times we were studying real; when we covered the Roman Empire, I saw him in a Roman toga, his hand in his jacket Napoleon style when we studied Napoleon. I don't remember how long he wore sandals—most likely till it got cold which it did early in the Midwest.

Trees

The first kind of trees many think of are red maples having
such a glorious blaze in the fall. They are believed to have
started in China about 120 million years ago and the glacier
periods isolating, encouraged over 180 species—more
kinds than are around now. The next are apple trees with
unforgettable spring beauty, a fragrance not forgotten

once it has been experienced. The pine stays green all year
so is very noticeable in white winter; one doesn't usually
notice they have brown needles under them. There are many
kinds such as the proud short needled Blue Spruce to the soft
long needled White Pine so prized in the lumbering era. Then

the graceful Weeping Willow that reminds one of girls with
long hair gossiping in the wind. Then what I call umbrella
trees that have the shape of umbrellas especially when
they lose their leaves; when in bloom they are spectacular seen
close or from a distance standing alone. You read that
the age of trees can be determined by growth ring—a way

also of telling what years had little rain. And the last is the
tree one had for climbing when young with convenient
low branches that invited exploration you claimed as your
own like you saw in pictures of explorers in your school
books claiming land. You bravely climbed just high enough

to see things differently—until climbing trees wasn't what
grown up girls did—but even then you felt an ownership.
When passing you began saying fewer and fewer words of
greeting as a sharp sadness decended making you bow your
head to hide tears.

Epilogue

Searching

for what we feel has been lost is universal:
did a confined Stephen Hawking exploring
space come the closest?

But another way (if we're brave enough)
could be to let go, free fall—finally look at
what's inside.

Acknowledgments

Blood Test in January: *In Hubble's Shadow* (Shanti Arts, 2017)

The Blue of Swimming Pools: Franklin-Christoph 2010 Poetry Contest Award Winner; *The Michigan Poet*, August , 2011; *Linq* December 2011

Defining Time: *In Hubble's Shadow* (Shanti Arts, 2017)

Dirt Roads: *In Hubble's Shadow* (Shanti Arts, 2017)

Dog Days Triptych: *A Matter of Selection* (Poetic Matrix Press, 2018)

Driving Into Town: *Postcard Poems and Prose Magazine*, July, 2018

Hanging Clothes on Clotheslines: *Red Earth Review,* Volume 6, 2018; *A Matter of Selection* (Poetic Matrix Press, 2018)

A Hardcover Book: T*he Society of Classical Poets,* November 6, 2017; *A Matter of Selection* (Poetic Matrix Press, 2018)

The Hovering: *Parentheses Journal* March 29, 2017; Peacock Journal, January 9, 2017

Our Unconscious Censor: *Vitamin ZZZ*, Summer, 2018

Passage Triptych: *The Literary Nest*, Spring, 2018

A Pink Cinquain: *Society of Classical Poets,* July, 2018

The Pleiades: *The Society of Classical Poets*, Vol. 5; Journal 2017; *Prisms, Particles, and Refractions* ((Finishing Line Press, 2017)

Shallow Boxes: *Better Than Starbucks*, December, 2017; *A Matter of Selection* (Poetic Matrix Press, 2018)

Shifting Continents: *Better Than Starbucks,* June 1, 2018

A Spider: *Prisms, Particles, and Refractions* (Finishing Line Press, 2017)

A Supermarket Triptych: *Dewpoint Literary Magazine*, 2019;

A Matter of Selection (Poetic Matrix Press, 2018)

There Were Only: *Heron Tree,* 2016; *Prisms, Particles, and Refractions* (Finishing Line Press, 2017)

Two Roads: *The Bunbury Creative Anthology*, Vol. 2, 2018

Questions of the Day: *The Blotter Magazine,* August, 2018

What Does it Mean? *Peacock Journal*, January 9, 2017; *A Matter of Selection* (Poetic Matrix Press, 2018); *In the Measuring* (Shanti Arts Press, 2018)

T-Shirts at Wendy's: *Spectrum*: University of California, Santa Barbara's College of Creative Studies, Vol. LXII, 2019

About the Author

Carol Smallwood has written or edited over five dozen books of poetry, creative nonfiction, nonfiction, and anthology. *Women on Poetry: Tips on Writing, Revising, Publishing and Teaching* is on Poets & Writers' List of Best Books for Writers. Recent anthologies include: *Genealogy and the Librarian: Perspectives on Research, Instruction, Outreach and Management* (McFarland, 2018); *Writing After Retirement: Tips by Successful Retired Writers* (Rowman & Littlefield, 2014); and *Bringing the Arts into the Library: An Outreach Handbook* (American Library Association, 2014).

Recent poetry collections include *Water, Earth, Air, Fire, and Picket Fences* (Lamar University Press, 2014); *Divining the Prime Meridian* (WordTech Editions, 2015); *In Hubble's Shadow* (Shanti Arts, 2017); *Prisms, Particles, and Refraction* (Finishing Line Press, 2017, nominated for the Society of Midland Authors Award in Poetry); and *A Matter of Selection* (Poetic Matrix Press, 2018); *Patterns: Moments in Time* (WordTech Collections, 2019). Her collection of poetry, fiction, and creative nonfiction, *Visits and Other Passages* (FinishingLine Press, 2019); her collection of essays, *Interweavings: Creative Nonfiction*, was published in 2017 (Shanti Arts). Smallwood, who has founded and supports humane societies, has received multiple Pushcart Prize nominations. She is in such references as *Who's Who in America; Who's Who in the World*; and *Wikipedia*. A multi-Pushcart nominee, recipient of the Albert Nelson Marquis Lifetime Achievement Award, she's a literary reader, judge, interviewer, who has founded humane societies.

www.ingramcontent.com/pod-product-compliance
Lightning Source LLC
Chambersburg PA
CBHW030850090426
42737CB00009B/1171